A ROOKIE'S GUIDE TO

RESEARCH

Second Edition

By

Barbara Mills

and

Mary Stiles

©1997 Union Creek Communications, Inc.
PO Box 1811
Bryson City, NC 28713

ISBN 0-9721404-0-9

Art work by John Fetterly

Additional copies of this publication
can be purchased through
Union Creek Communications
(828) 488-3596
FAX: (828) 488-1018

Foreword

    A Rookie's Guide to Research, as its name indicates, is written particularly for the novice researcher--

someone who has had little or no previous experience in this area. Although students can use the guide

independent of any further instructor input, a classroom setting with teacher guidance, assistance, and

encouragement is still the ideal way to assure a firm foundation in research skills. For those students who have

had this initial guidance, the Rookie's Guide is an excellent tool to refresh and reinforce previous learning. Even

the experienced researcher can turn to the readily accessible documentations and find bibliographic help for all

but the most technical areas. In most cases, citations follow MLA guidelines.

About the Authors

Barbara Mills is a media specialist with over 25 years of experience. She holds a Master's degree in Educational Technology and a Bachelor of Arts degree in English and Social Studies from Western Carolina University.

Mary Stiles is an English teacher with over 30 years experience She holds an advanced degree (Ed.S.) in English along with a Bachelor's and Master's degree in English from Western Carolina University.

Both educators have had considerable experience in teaching and directing students in research projects. This publication is an outgrowth of their joint efforts to enable students to become more astute researchers.

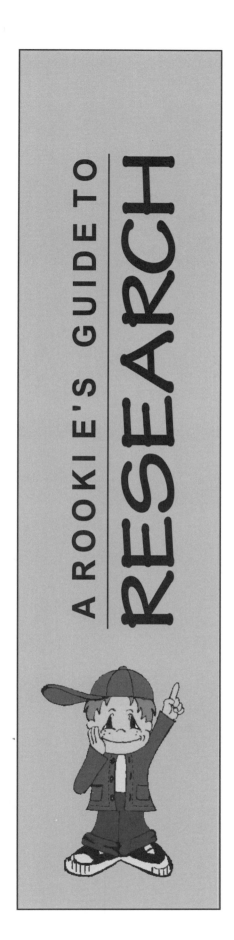

A ROOKIE'S GUIDE TO RESEARCH

Table of Contents

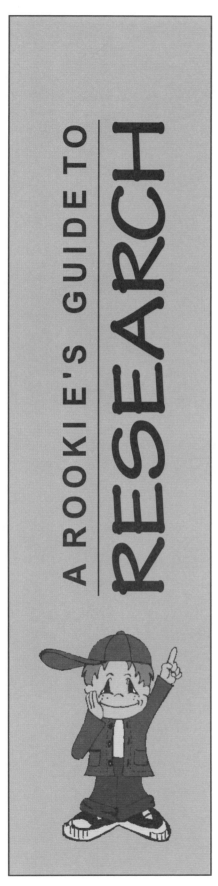

A ROOKIE'S GUIDE TO
RESEARCH

The Research Process

This chapter will help you

The Research Process
Steps

A research paper is nonfiction writing relying on information obtained from personal experience and observation or on information gathered from the knowledge of others. Most beginning researchers use information written by others to explore a subject

Steps

Steps in developing a research paper:

1. Select and narrow a subject.

2. Make a list of questions to answer. (These will form the basis for an outline and a thesis sentence.)   Identify key words within the questions to use as possible search terms.

3. Develop a preliminary thesis (theme) statement expressing the central idea of your paper; expect to revise it after a significant amount of research has been completed.

4. Compile a working list of sources (the list of works cited) to investigate.

5. Read - read - read and take notes - and more notes.

6. Prepare, alphabetize and type the list of works cited using proper formats.   You may revise the list later if you choose additional sources.

7. Arrange notes in some appropriate order to make an outline.

8. Revise your thesis statement and update your list of works cited entries.

9. Use notes and outline to write a first draft, documenting from the list of works cited as you write.

10. Revise your first draft.

11. Utilize the writer's checklist on page 75 to check your paper for errors. Make changes wherever necessary.

12. Type the final draft of your paper.

The Research Process
Topic • Thesis

Topic

Selecting a topic/subject

Your instructor will either assign you a topic to research or let you choose one. Keep two things in mind when deciding: the time you have in which to do the paper and the required length. You usually start with a general topic and narrow it. For instance, suppose you are assigned *Diseases* as a topic. Large books have been written about this topic, so the subject must be narrowed:

Diseases (too large)

to

Diseases Transmitted by Animals (still too large)

to

Rocky Mountain Spotted Fever (a possibility)

Thesis

The Thesis Sentence unifies the paper; it brings everything together. It lets you know where you are headed and keeps you on the right track.

Let's go back to Diseases. Assume you have decided to do your paper on the many characteristics of Rocky Mountain Spotted Fever. Everything you read and take notes on should, in some way, support this viewpoint. Some instructors/writers prefer the researcher to use a thesis sentence that leaves no doubt about the topic.

The thesis, usually stated in the final sentence of the introductory paragraph, might read: "This paper will define and give statistics about Rocky Mountain Spotted Fever; describe its symptoms, diagnosis and treatment; and relate preventive measures and the future outlook of the disease." As you gain experience in writing, you will want to refine the thesis to something less concrete which still expresses the overall viewpoint of your paper. A thesis for the above topic might read: "Rocky Mountain Spotted Fever is an acute, infectious disease which can be effectively treated and possibly prevented."

Works Cited

The preliminary list of works cited is a list of books, magazines, and other sources that have some possible information on your topic. At this stage, go to the library to begin your research by compiling this list. Use your knowledge of the library to look in appropriate places--and make the librarian your best friend.

Many instructors require students to write their list of works cited information on note cards; others allow students to write their source information in a notebook. Whichever method you choose, you must include information to cover the following bibliographic entries and possibly others: books, periodicals, reference books, interviews, reprints, and electronic sources such as CD-ROM sources and Internet sources. *Writing down all the information concerning your sources the first time will save you time and energy later on.*

The following note cards give examples of the type of information required for common works cited cards. The information on these cards will form the basis of the list of works cited in your the research paper. (See pages 53 and 70 for examples.) For help on citing sources which are not illustrated here, please refer to the section of this book on **Documentation** beginning on page 17 which presents the information required for works cited entries.

Works Cited Card for a book

> Kotre, John, and Elizabeth Hall. *Seasons of Life: Our Dramatic Journey From Birth to Death.* Boston: Little, 1990.

The works cited card for books should include the author, title, place of publication, publisher and date of publication. All of this data should be taken from the front and reverse side of the title page.

The Research Process
Works Cited Cards

Magazine

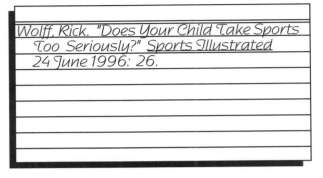

Wolff, Rick. "Does Your Child Take Sports
Too Seriously?" Sports Illustrated
24 June 1996: 26.

Magazine articles require the author of the article (if given), the title of the article, the title of the magazine, its date of publication and the page number of the article.

Newspaper

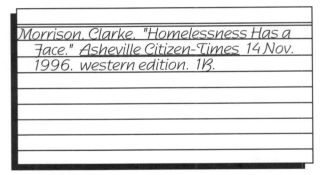

Morrison, Clarke. "Homelessness Has a
Face." Asheville Citizen-Times 14 Nov.
1996. western edition. 1B.

Newspaper articles require the author (if given), the title of the article, the name of the newspaper, the date of publication, the edition, and the page number and section where the article can be found.

CD-ROM database which is periodically updated

Carvell, Tim. "The Big Business of March
Madness: Economics of the NCAA's
Men's College Basketball Tournament."
Fortune 1 Apr. 1996: 35. InfoTrac:
SuperTOM+. CD-ROM. Information
Access Company. Sept. 1996.

CD-ROM databases require the full information for the original source of the information, the title of the database, publication medium, CD-ROM publisher, and date of publication of the CD-ROM.

Taking notes

Gathering information

You are now ready to begin gathering information about your topic. This is the place where you will spend most of your research time--reading and taking notes. Taking notes is **NOT** opening a book and writing exactly what you find there. Normally, you will read a short section and then summarize or paraphrase what you want to remember; in other words, you will put the information into your own words. If you do find information that is vital to your paper and you believe you should include it exactly the way it is written in the source, you must cite it as a direct quotation, enclosing it in quotation marks.

Instructors sometimes allow students leeway in the manner of notetaking. Some teachers require the researcher to write the notes on index cards; others allow the researcher to write in notebooks or to use loose-leaf paper that can be rearranged easily. Whichever way you choose, be certain to include enough information at the very beginning of each note card to indicate the source of the information; usually the author's name, the title of the book or article, and the page number referenced are enough.

It is most helpful to categorize the information as you make notes. For example, if you are writing a note about the symptoms of Rocky Mountain Spotted Fever, make a note on the card that this data relates to "symptoms". This category (also known as a slug) is created by the researcher in order to sort information. For example, disease categories might include causes, care and treatment, symptoms, and current research. When you finish your notetaking, you can then separate your cards into these categories, thus forming the divisions of your outline. Below is an example of a note card.

Author	*Moore and Quick*
One fact taken from the source	*Rapid onset of fever occurs in almost all patients followed by a rash in 85 % to 90% of infected people.*
Page number, if given	*n.p. (CD-ROM)*
Category (Slug)	*Symptoms*

The Research Process
Using Note Cards

Using note cards

- Continue to make note cards similar to the sample card, being careful to include all of the necessary data.

- Exhaust all of the data from one source before going on to another source.

- When you move to a different source, make note cards only for new facts that you have not already included in your notes.

- When you have made notes from all of your sources, sort your cards into the categories which you previously defined. For example, place all of the cards dealing with "symptoms" in one stack and all of the cards dealing with "care and treatment" in another stack.

- Some cards may not fit into a category or you may not have enough cards in a category to form a stack. Put these aside. You may find a use for these in your introduction or conclusion.

- Sort the cards in each category into a logical sequence. Decide which one should come first, second, and so forth. If holes in your research appear, go back to the library for additional information. Each section of cards should be about equal in number. You should have enough cards to cover your topic thoroughly.

- The cards you have placed in the categories will become the body of your research paper. You can now develop your outline, using the categories you have defined as the main topics.

Outlining

An **outline** gives direction to your paper. Here, too, requirements may differ. The outline usually evolves during the reading-researching stage of the paper. The beginning outline is really a working one--a starting point from which to build. Of course, whatever is put into the outline must, in some way, relate to your thesis sentence. Sometimes this means eliminating information you have gathered.

As you continue to research, connections between the information you find will begin to surface. Bring these connections together under some general heading. Making a good outline usually takes time and effort. Normally, you will revise several times; however, the better the outline, the easier it will be to write your paper. When an outline is required, the form must be consistent. That means, if you have a Roman numeral **I**, you must have a **II**; if you have an **A**, you must have a **B**.

Outline order

The following example shows the correct order:

I.

    A.

        l.

            a.

                (l)

                    (a)

                    (b)

                (2)

            b.

        2.

    B.

II.

In high school, very seldom will you need to use an outline this detailed. Usually the levels of Roman numeral **I**, capital **A**, and number **l** are sufficient. *See sample outlines on pages 47 and 59.*

The Research Process
In-text Citations

Plagiarism

It is not sufficient simply to gather your information and put it into a paper. You must also give credit to the person whose work you use; otherwise, you will probably be guilty of **plagiarism.** Plagiarism can be defined as using another person's writings or ideas as if they were your own. When you plagiarize, you let the reader believe the ideas presented are yours when they actually belong to someone else. By the time you are in college, the penalties for plagiarism range from failure for the paper to failure for the whole course to even expulsion from school. Avoiding plagiarism is easy: simply give credit to the author of the information. This means that most of your paper will be documented; after all, it is a research paper relying on the information of others to support your thesis sentence.

Signal phrase

Documentation is usually accomplished through in-text citations; this is also referred to as parenthetical documentation. A **signal phrase** is often used to introduce source material. A signal phrase leads into the source by citing the author's last name at the beginning of the sentence. If you use signal phrases to introduce documented information, you need only cite the page number of the book or magazine where you found the data. The following example illustrates the use of a signal phrase:

> Scruggs points out that little music has ever been written for the banjo; many of
>
> the tunes and playing techniques were handed down by banjo players through the
>
> generations (10).

"Scruggs points out" is the signal phrase used to introduce the cited material. The number (10) shown in parentheses in the in-text citation is the page number where the information is located in the original source. The complete publication information for the material cited will be found at the end of the paper in the alphabetical list of works cited in an entry beginning with *Scruggs*. The signal phrase points the reader to the following reference in the list of works cited:

> Scruggs, Earl. <u>Earl Scruggs and the 5-String Banjo</u>. New York: Peer International,
>
> 1968.

This same information can also be referenced without the use of a signal phrase. If you do not mention the author's name in the text, you must give the author's name at the end of the information you reference. The information might look like this:

> Little music has ever been written for the banjo; many of the tunes and playing
>
> techniques were handed down by banjo players through the generations
>
> (Scruggs 10).

Both methods point the reader to the entry in the list of works cited where the entire publication information may be found. Notice that in both cases, the period follows the in-text citation.

If an author's name is not given, begin the citation with the word the entry is alphabetized by in the list of works cited. If more than one article has the same word or words at the beginning of a citation, additional words must be added to identify the source. If an entire paragraph of information comes from the same source--and the same page(s)--document the information only once at the end of the paragraph unless you are documenting a direct quotation which should be cited immediately after the quotation. Even though the next paragraph of information might come from the same source, it is usually a good idea to document each paragraph so that there will be no misunderstanding concerning where the information came from.

Direct quotations

When citing word-for-word **quotations**, be sure that the quotation matches the source exactly; it should be identical to the source. Quotations provide credibility for what you are saying; you support your point by quoting an authority. When you **paraphrase,** you match the source in terms of meaning but put it into your own words. Paraphrasing shows that you have command of the material without being a slave to the original author's words. In a **summary** you simply use your own words to sum up the central point; thus, a summary is much shorter than the source itself. Summaries are good for expressing the main idea of someone else's work while avoiding unnecessary details. In either case, you must document the source of your information through in-text citations and in the list of works cited. Although there are some fine points in certain cases of parenthetical documentation, the information presented here is basically all you need for high school and lower-level college courses.

The Research Process
Rough Draft

Rough Draft

Drafting the Paper

After you have gathered your information, reviewed it, polished your thesis sentence, and made your outline, you are ready to write.

▶ Type the list of works cited, being careful to use the correct format. An example of the correct format can be found on pages 53 and 70. Typing the *Works Cited* page first makes the in-text citations (the citations found in the body of the paper) much easier. Examples of in-text citations can be found in the research papers and in the chapter on documentation.

▶ Use your outline to compose the rough draft:

- Organize research to follow your outline.

- Write the body of the paper before writing the introduction and conclusion if this is easier for you.

- Begin each paragraph with a topic sentence relating to your thesis sentence and use facts to support the topic sentence.

- Include the in-text citations as you write; detailed information concerning this step begins on page 10.

- If you did not do this previously, write an introductory paragraph explaining your topic and stating the thesis.

▶ Revise your rough draft as necessary

- Go over your paper and take out anything that doesn't seem to support your thesis sentence.

- Fill in obvious "empty spots"--even if you must return to the library for further research.

- Make certain the points you have presented are supported by evidence.

- Read the paper aloud to yourself, listening carefully to the wording; change the wording wherever necessary to insure that the words flow smoothly and that the thoughts are unified.

- Add appropriate transitional words and phrases. A list of these words may be found on page 79.

- Use the writer's check list on page 75.

- Run a spell check.

- Have someone else read your paper for correct content, clarity, spelling and grammar.

Final Draft

▶ Complete the final draft of your paper--the one you will hand in.

- Proofread your paper one last time for any mistakes.

- Make an extra copy of your paper to keep for reference since many teachers keep student papers on file for a period of time.

- Follow the directions of the instructor as to placing the document in a report folder.

The Research Process
Format

General Guidelines

Format of a Research Paper

Typing: Make sure that you use a computer or typewriter with clear print; do not use script fonts. Fonts should be 12 point and easily readable. *Times, Times New Roman* or *Helvetica* are acceptable fonts. Print or write on one side of the paper only. If your instructor will accept handwritten work, make certain that it is neat, readable, and written in dark blue or black ink.

EVERYTHING should be **double-spaced** throughout the paper. *This includes the outline and list of works cited.* Long quotations are double-spaced and are indented 10 spaces from the left margin. Omit quotation marks when using long indented quotations.

Do **not** use ALL CAPITAL letters for the document title or for the list of works cited.

Margins

Margins: Leave one-inch margins at the top and bottom of each sheet of paper as well as one-inch margins on the right and left hand sides of the paper. The header including the page number should be set one-half inch from the top of the paper.

Title Page

Title Page: A separate title page is not necessary for a research paper. Instead, place the information that would usually appear on the title page on the first page of your paper. Beginning one inch from the top and flush with the left margin, type your name; double space, type your instructor's name; double space, type the title of the course; double space, and then type the date. The date should begin with the day, the month, and the year . (Example: 11 April 1996) Double space again and center the title of your paper. **Do not underline the title; do not put it in all caps, and do not put quotation marks around it**. Finally, double space once more. Begin at the left margin; indent five spaces, and you are ready to begin the body of your paper. *See samples on pages 49 and 61.*

If your instructor requires a title page, the following format is suggested: center the title of the paper in the middle of the page; skip two lines and center the word *by*; skip two more lines and center your name. About two-thirds down the page, center the title of the course; skip two lines and center the instructor's name; skip two more lines and center the date. If you are using a word processing program, check the placement of the data by choosing "Print Preview", making adjustments as necessary. *See sample title pages on pages 45 and 57.*

Length of paper

Length: Most instructors set a minimum number of pages--and sometimes a maximum. In reality, like all writing, it is not its length--nor lack of it--that makes a successful paper, but what is said and how.

Page Numbers

Page Numbers: Number the pages throughout your paper in the upper right-hand corner, one-half inch from the top and one inch from the right edge of the paper. Your last name should appear before the page number. Do **not** put a **p.** before a number or a period after one. Begin numbering on the first page of text continuing through the list of works cited.

Works Cited

The list of works cited format: The list of works cited comes at the end of the paper and begins on a new page. Number each page of the list of works cited continuing the numbers from the text of the paper. Come down one inch and center the title: *Works Cited*. The words *Works Cited* should be in plain text, not in bold or italics. They should **not** be in all capital letters **nor** in larger letters than the rest of the text. Double space between the title and the first entry. The entries are to be entered **alphabetically** by the author's last name. If the author's name is not given, alphabetize by the first major word of the text, omitting *A, An,* and *The.* Each entry should start at the left margin; additional lines for that entry should be indented five spaces from the left margin. Double space between each line of the entry and between each entry. See samples on pages 53 and 70.

A ROOKIE'S GUIDE TO RESEARCH

Documentation

This chapter will help you cite and document

Documentation Guidelines

Creating a proper listing for a *Works Cited* page or giving credit to authors of the information is often a difficult experience for novice researchers. To make this experience less painful, we have gathered information from a variety of sources and have given examples of how this data should be cited in the list of works cited and within the body of the paper.

Be sure to follow the punctuation exactly as it is shown in the works cited entries: periods, commas, underlines, colons, etc. Note the placement of the end punctuation in the in-text citations. The period or end punctuation generally follows the in-text citations.

The World Wide Web is an ever-changing medium containing a wide variety of sources. These sources range from general websites containing text information to on-line radio and television news and sports sites complete with photographs, movie clips and sound clips. Because new formats are constantly being added, it is difficult to cite these sources in a standard format. Utilizing MLA style, we have sought to make these entries and in-text citations as simple as possible for the novice researcher. Remember to cite the original source of the material as completely as possible based on the available bibliographic information; then cite the available website data. Use care to follow the rules of fair use of copyrighted data. When in doubt, e-mail the website editor for permission to use materials found on the site in question.

Book with one author

Works Cited Entry:

Twain, Mark. <u>The Adventures of Huckleberry Finn</u>. Cleveland: World, 1947.

Author. Title. Place of Publication. Publisher. Date of Publication.

In-text Citation:

The book ends with Huck remarking that he has no intentions of becoming civilized

(Twain 377).

<u>Twain</u> refers to the author's last name and <u>377</u> is the page number where the information is located.

Additional book by the same author

If another book by the same author follows this entry in the list of works cited, the author's name should be replaced with three hyphens as in the example which follows:

- - -. <u>The Adventures of Tom Sawyer</u>. Boston: Houghton, 1962.

Documentation
Books

Book with two authors

Works Cited Entry:

Kotre, John, and Elizabeth Hall. <u>Seasons of Life: Our Dramatic Journey From Birth</u>

<u>to Death</u>. Boston: Little, 1990.

Authors. (First name listed is reversed; second is in order) Title. Place of
Publication. Publisher. Date of Publication.

In-text Citation:

• **When authors are mentioned in the signal phrase:**

Kotre and Hall state that "most young people emerge from high school with only a

hazy idea of what their future occupation might entail" (168).

When authors are named in the text, you need only cite the page numbers
as shown above.

• **When authors are not mentioned in a signal phrase:**

Teenagers often do not have clear occupational concepts when they leave high

school. (Kotre and Hall 168).

Book with three authors

Works Cited Entry:

Smolan, Rich, Phillip Moffitt, and Matthew Naythons. <u>Ancient Arts and Modern</u>

<u>Medicine</u>.   New York: Prentice, 1990.

Authors. (First name listed in reverse order; second and third names are
in regular order) Title. Place of publication. Publisher. Date of
Publication.

In-text Citation:

"Women have always been healers, and in traditional cultures, women are often the

principal healers - the first resort against illness or disease" (Smolan, Moffitt, and

Naythons 85).

Book with more than three authors

Works Cited Entry:

Ericksson, Bengt O., et al. <u>Sports Medicine: Health and Medication</u>. New York:

Facts on File, 1990.

*First author. Abbreviation **et al**. (meaning "and others") Title. Place of
publication. Publisher, Date of Publication.*

In-text Citation:

Physical exercise can provoke an asthmatic attack in an asthmatic who is otherwise

symptom-free (Eriksson et al. 66).

Book with an editor when the entire book is used

Works Cited Entry:

Asby, Ruth, and Deborah Gore Ohrn, eds. <u>Herstory: Women Who Changed</u>

<u>History</u>. New York: Viking, 1994.

*Author/s. Editor designation (eds.) Title of book. Place of Publication.
Publisher. Date of Publication.*

*If no author is given or if reference is given to more than one article,
place the editor in the author position. However, if only one
article with an author is used, the author of the article comes in
the author position with the editor following the title of the book.
See sample in "Citing a selection within a multivolume work".*

In-text Citation:

Queen Isabella I had a disagreement with her brother Enrique over whom she was

to marry. He had arranged for her to marry someone he had chosen, but she

wished to marry her second cousin Ferdinand, a marriage which would have great

political potential (Asby and Ohrn 40).

Documentation
Books

Book by a corporate author

Works Cited

> Reader's Digest. New Fix-It-Yourself Manual. Pleasantville, NY: Reader's Digest,
>
> 1996.
>
> *Corporate author. Title. Place of Publication. Publisher. Date of*
> *Publication.*

In-text Citation:

> Excessive cleaning of a VCR may damage its heads. A VCR that is used frequently or is
>
> subjected to poor quality tapes will require cleaning more often (Reader's 352).

Book with an anonymous author

Works Cited Entry:

> Occupational Outlook Handbook. 1992-93 ed. Auburn, CA: CFKR Career Materials,
>
> 1992.
>
> *Title of book. Place of Publication. Publisher. Date of Publication.*

In-text Citation:

> Each state requires people who practice law to be admitted to its bar or to be
>
> licensed to practice law (Occupational 102).

In-text Citation with a signal phrase:

> The Occupational Outlook Handbook states that each state requires people who
>
> practice law to be admitted to its bar or to be licensed to practice law (102).

Work in an anthology (a collection of writings)

Works Cited Entry:

Daniels, Jonathan. "Tar Heels All." <u>Discovering North Carolina</u>. Eds. Jack

Claiborne and William Price. Chapel Hill: UNC P., 1991. 99-101.

Author of work in anthology. Name of work in anthology. Title of book. Edited by. Place of publication. Publisher. Date of Publication. Page numbers.

In-text Citation:

". . . there were only two classes of people, those who never had worn shoes and

those who made you feel that you never had" (Daniels 99).

An introduction, preface, foreword or afterword

Works Cited Entry:

Moore, Christopher. Introduction. <u>Selected Poems of Henry Wadsworth

Longfellow</u>. By Henry Wadsworth Longfellow. New York: Gramercy,

1992. 7-8.

Author of introduction, preface, etc. Title of piece quoted. Title of book. Author of book. Place of publication. Publisher. Date of Publication. Page numbers.

In-text Citation:

Born on February 27, 1807, in Portland, Maine, Longfellow counted a long,

distinguished line of upperclass New Englanders in his lineage (Moore 7).

Documentation
Books

Volume in a multivolume work; most volumes used

Works Cited Entry:

Irving, David. <u>Hitler's War</u>. 2 vols. New York: Viking, 1977.

Author or editor. Title of multivolumed work. Number of volumes in series. Place of publication. Publisher. Date of publication.

In-text Citation:

At the last Eva Braun was "pale but composed," wearing a blue dress with white trimmings and a favorite gold bracelet which "meant a lot" to her (Irving 2:901).

Cite both the volume and the page number.

Multivolume work: Each volume with a different title

Works Cited Entry:

Catton, Bruce. <u>The Coming Fury</u>. Garden City, NY: Doubleday, 1961. Vol. 1 of <u>The Centennial History of the Civil War</u>. 3 vols. 1961-1965.

Author. Title. Place of Publication. Publisher. Date of Publication. Vol. Number. Title of the Series of Books. Number of books in the series. Inclusive dates of publication for series.

In-text Citation:

Most of the soldiers had not fought at all. Some looked forward to battle as one would look forward to participating in a sport (Catton 410).

A selection within a multivolume work

Works Cited Entry:

> Holladay, Hal. "Crazy Horse." <u>Great Lives From History: American Series</u>. Ed.
>
> Frank N. Magill. Vol. 2. Pasadena, CA: Salem, 1987. 5 vols.
>
> *Author of selection. Title of selection. Title of book. Editor. Volume used.*
> *Place of publication. Publisher. Date of publication. Total*
> *number of volumes in the series.*

In-text Citation:

> When Crazy Horse was twelve, he killed his first buffalo and rode a newly captured
>
> horse. Subsequently he was called "His Horse Looking" (Holladay 565).
>
> *You need only cite the page number if you use only one volume of the*
> *multivolume work; otherwise, cite the volume number also.*

Article in a familiar reference book (e.g. encyclopedia)

With author given

Works Cited Entry:

> Adams, Charles. "Islam." <u>Encyclopedia Americana</u>. 1993 ed.
>
> *Author of article. Name of article. Name of reference book. Date of*
> *edition.*

In-text Citation:

> The city of Mecca organized two annual caravans; each citizen from the poorest to
>
> the most wealthy was allowed to invest in these ventures (Adams 492).

With no author given

Works Cited Entry:

> "Harmonica." <u>Encyclopedia International</u>. 1981 ed.
>
> *Title of article. Name of reference book. Date of edition.*

In-text Citation:

> Credit for the invention of the harmonica in 1821 is usally given to Friedrich
>
> Buschmann of Berlin ("Harmonica" 306).

Documentation
Books

Unfamiliar reference book

Works Cited Entry:

Hickok, Ralph. The Encyclopedia of North American Sports History. New York:

Facts On File, 1991.

Author. Title of book. Place of publication. Publisher. Date of
Publication.

In-text Citation:

Due to an accident which injured his right index finger, his thumb and middle

finger, "Three Finger" Mordecai P. C. Brown had to alter his pitching technique so

that his fastball became a sinker, enabling him to become one of the best pitchers in

baseball (Hickok 85).

Pamphlet

Works Cited Entry:

Rankin, Hugh F. North Carolina in the American Revolution.   Raleigh, NC: State

Department of Archives and History, 1959.

Author of pamphlet. Name of pamphlet. Place of publication. Publisher.
Date of publication.

If no author is given, begin with the title of the pamphlet.

In-text Citation:

Since money was a critical problem for the new state, North Carolina followed the

example of other new states and began to issue paper money (Rankin 27).

Newspaper

Works Cited Entry:

Morrison, Clarke. "Homelessness Has a Face." <u>Asheville Citizen-Times</u> 14 Nov.

1996, western ed.: B1.

*Author of article. Name of Article. Name of Newspaper. Date. Edition, if
listed on the masthead. Page number and section of article.*

In-text Citation:

Recent surveys show that "34 percent of homeless men seeking refuge in shelters are

veterans" (Morrison B1).

Monthly magazine

Works Cited Entry:

Clifford, Mary Louise. "Keeper of the Light." <u>American History</u> Sept.-Oct. 1996:

24-28.

*Author of article. Name of article. Name of periodical. Date. Page
number/s of article. (Do not place a period after the name of the
magazine).*

In-text Citation:

Sons, wives and daughters learned to keep the lighthouse lights burning and often

replaced the men lighthouse keepers if they became disabled or died (Clifford 24).

Documentation
Periodicals

Weekly magazine

Works Cited Entry:

Wolff, Rick. "Does Your Child Take Sports Too Seriously?" <u>Sports Illustrated</u> 24

June 1996: 26.

Author of article. Name of Article. Name of Periodical. Day, Month, and Year of the article (in that order) without punctuation for weekly publications. Page number of article.

In-text Citation:

For most kids, the disappointment of being on a losing team lasts only a few

minutes; they are quick to realize that there will be a new game on another day

(Wolff 26).

Article with interrupted page numbers

Works Cited Entry:

Martin, Michael. "Mountain Legend." <u>American History</u> Sept.-Oct. 1996: 36+.

For an entry where the page numbers do not follow consecutively, use a plus sign after the page number to indicate a break in the numbering sequence.

In-text Citation

The preceding Works Cited entry should be cited internally the same way as the other magazine articles.

In the event that no author of the article is given, begin with the first major word of the title of the article.

Scholarly journal

Works Cited Entry:

Mazer, Norma Fox. "Silent Censorship." School Library Journal 42.8 (1996): 42.

Author of article. Title of article. Title of periodical. Volume number. Issue number. Year of publication. Page number/s of entire article.

In-text Citation:

"By cancelling my visit out of fear of possible trouble, they sent a strong signal of giving in to censors . . ."(Mazer 42).

Article on microfiche

Works Cited Entry:

Furlong, William Barry. "The Panther at the Plate." The New York Times 21 Sept. 1958: sec. 6: 43. Great Personalities Two as Reported in The New York Times (1981): fiche 1, grids 9-10.

Author of article. Title of article. Periodical. Date. Section. Page. Source of microfiche. Date of microfiche publication. Number of microfiche. Grids on which article appears.

In-text Citation:

When asked about his success as a batter, Aaron replied, "Whatever I'm doin', I don't want to know what it is. I just want to keep on doin' it" (Furlong).

Documentation
Periodicals

Reprint of magazine article

Works Cited Entry:

Chanute, Octave. "The Wright Brothers' Flights." <u>Independent</u> 4 June 1908: n.

pag. Rpt. in <u>1905-1915 The Progressive Era</u>. Chicago: Encyclopaedia

Britannica, 1968. Vol. 13 of <u>The Annals of America</u>. 118-120.

Author of original article. Original article title. Work the article
originally appeared in. Date of the work. Page number of
original work. **Rpt. in** *name of current work the article*
appears in along with complete bibliographic info for that title
followed by the page numbers of current source.

In-text Citation:

On May 14, Wilbur Wright alone made a flight of eight miles at the speed of forty-

five miles an hour. The flight ended in a wreck behind a sand dune (Chanute

119).

Article reprinted in loose-leaf collection of articles (e.g. SIRS)

Works Cited Entry

Wassermann, Selma. "What Can Schools Become?" <u>Phi Delta Kappan</u> June 1984:

690+. <u>School</u>. Ed. Eleanor Goldstein. Vol. 3. Boca Raton, FL: SIRS,

1989. Art. 15.

Cite the information for the first publication followed by the information
for the publication containing the reprinted data.

In-text Citation

According to Albert Einstein, "Creativity is far more consequential than knowledge

in furthering the significant advances of humankind" (Wassermann).

Book Review

Works Cited

Lambert, Pam. "Cause of Death." Rev. of <u>Cause of Death</u> by Patricia D. Cornwell.

<u>People Weekly</u> 1 July 1996: 30.

*Author of review. Name of article. Name and author of book reviewed.
Periodical. Date of periodical. Page number.*

In-text Citation

". . . the author and Scarpetta are doing what they do best--using forensic science's

ever expanding wizardry to help the dead tell their tales" (Lambert 30).

Movie Review

Works Cited Entry

Johnson, Brian D. "A Time to Kill." Rev. of <u>A Time to Kill</u> dir. Joel Schumacher.

<u>Macleans</u> 5 Aug. 1996: 50.

*Author of review. Name of article. Name or movie reviewed. Director of
movie. Periodical. Date of periodical. Page number.*

In-text Citation

The film "sanctifies everything that is alarming about the American justice system--

all in the name of honest entertainment" (Johnson 50).

Documentation
Miscellaneous

Interview

Works Cited Entry

Humphrey, John. Personal interview. 27 Oct. 1994.

McMillan, Janice. Telephone interview. 18 Feb. 1992.

Name of person being interviewed. Type of interview. Date of interview
with the day coming first.

In-text Citation

John Humphrey stated that the transition from work to retirement is not always a

healthy one (Humphrey).

Television and Radio Programs

Works Cited Entry

Good Morning America. American Broadcasting Company. WJLA, Washington,

DC. 20 Mar. 1997.

Name of program. Company producing program. Television station
airing program. Date of program.

In-text Citation

Even more recently, during a television appearance, a forensic handwriting

expert, discussing a case in the news today in which a ransom note is involved,

stated that, though many similarities exist, handwriting evidence is very often

being considered "inconclusive" (Good Morning).

Periodical article on CD-ROM database (e.g. Info-Trac) which is regularly updated

Works Cited Entry:

Carvell, Tim. "The Big Business of March Madness: Economics of the NCAA's

Men's College Basketball Tournament." <u>Fortune</u> 1 Apr. 1996: 35.

<u>InfoTrac: SuperTOM+</u>. CD-ROM. Information Access. Sept. 1996.

Publication information for print source (author, title, date, etc.). Title of the Database (underlined). Publication Medium (CD-ROM). Name of Vendor.. Electronic Publication Date.

In-text Citation:

Even though CBS has paid the NCAA $1.725 billion for the rights to the men's

college basketball championships through the year 2002, they will actually come

out in the black by $20 million on the tournament this year (Carvell).

Reference book article on up-dated CD-ROM database

Works Cited Entry:

Mohr, James C. "Abortion." <u>The Reader's Companion to American History</u>. 1991

ed. Houghton, 1991. <u>InfoTrac: SuperTOM+</u>. CD-ROM. Information

Access. April 1996.

Publication information for print source (Author, title, place of publication, etc.). Title of the Database (Underlined). Publication Medium (CD-ROM). Name of Vendor. Electronic Publication Date.

In-text Citation:

Abortion was legal under colonial common law and remained legal under

American common law provided that the pregnancy was terminated before

quickening--the first perception of movement of the fetus by the mother (Mohr).

Documentation
CD-ROMs

News service article on up-dated CD-ROM database

Works Cited Entry:

Ager, Susan. "Decision to Abort Never Easily Made." <u>Knight-Ridder/Tribune News</u>

<u>Service</u> 14 Aug. 1996. <u>InfoTrac: SuperTOM+</u>. CD-ROM. Information

Access. Nov. 1996.

*Publication information for print source (Author, title, etc.) Title of the
Database (Underlined). Publication Medium (CD-ROM). Name
of Vendor. Electronic Publication Date.*

In-text Citation:

A 10-year study of high school students in Wisconsin revealed that "only one in

three children had daily conversations with their parents . . . half the parents

admitted they neither knew their children's friends nor what their kids did after

school" (Ager).

Selection from Nonperiodical CD-ROM database

Works Cited Entry:

"Introduction to Anne Bradstreet." <u>Monarch Notes for Windows</u>. CD-ROM.

Parsippany, NJ: Bureau of Electronic Publishing, 1993.

*Some CD-ROM databases are not routinely updated. Cite these electronic
sources similar to the way you would a book, being careful to
add the publication medium.*

*Article. Name of CD-ROM database (underlined). Medium. Place of
Publication. Publisher. Date of Publication.*

In-text Citation:

The most important kind of reading for the early settlers was religious books

followed by history and books on conduct, domestic relations, politics and the

professions ("Introduction").

Court Case on CD-ROM

Works Cited Entry

Alexander v. United States. 509 U.S. 544. U. S. Supreme Ct. 1993. Rpt. in <u>SIRS</u>

<u>Government Reporter</u>. CD-ROM. Boca Raton, FL: SIRS, 1994.

Court case. Vol. of Code. Division of ruling. Page number of case. Court that made the ruling. Year of the decision. Reprint information for the CD-ROM source.

Note: The name of the case is not underlined in the Works Cited, but it is underlined in the text of the paper.

In-text Citation

The case of <u>Alexander v. United States</u> deals with free speech and speaks to the

term "prior restraint" (Alexander).

Computer Diskette

Works Cited Entry

"Long Description for Automotive Technician." <u>Discover</u>. Ver. 5.11. Diskette.

ACT, 1993.

Author (if given). Title of the selection. Title of the computer program (underlined). Version. Publication medium (Ex. diskette). City of publication. Publisher. Year of publication.

If you cannot find some of the information, cite only what is available.

In-text Citation

Automotive technicians should have mechanical aptitude, problem solving ability

along with an understanding of electronics, mathematics and hydraulics ("Long").

Documentation
CD-ROMs

Reprint of a book selection on CD-ROM

Individual CD-ROM

Works Cited Entry

Conrad, Joseph. "To H. G. Wells." 4 Dec. 1898 in his <u>Joseph Conrad: Life and</u>

        <u>Letters</u>. Ed. G. Jean Aubry. Vol. 1. Doubleday, 1927. 259-60. Rpt. in

        <u>Discovering Authors</u>. CD-ROM. Detroit: Gale, 1993.

*The full bibliographic data for the original work, followed by the words
"Rpt. in" followed by the bibliographic data for the CD-ROM.*

Networked CD-ROM

*If you are working on a network which does not allow physical access to the
bibliographic data for the CD-ROM, you may cite the above entry
as follows:*

Conrad, Joseph. "To H. G. Wells." 4 Dec. 1898 in his <u>Joseph Conrad: Life and</u>

        <u>Letters</u>. Ed. G. Jean Aubry. Vol. 1. Doubleday, 1927. 259-60. Rpt. in

        <u>Discovering Authors.</u> Vers. 1.0. 1993. Electronic. Marianna Black Public

        Lib., Bryson City, NC. 15 Nov. 1998.

*Give the full bibliographic entry for the source. Name of database (under-
lined) Version if available. The word "Electronic." Physical
location of the network. Date you accessed the database.*

In-text Citation

In speaking of the genius of H. G. Wells, Joseph Conrad asserts that "If it [<u>The</u>

<u>Invisible Man</u>] just misses being tremendous, it is because you didn't make it so--and

if you didn't, there isn't a man in England who could" (Conrad).

General Website on the World Wide Web (WWW)

Works Cited Entry

Axton, Myles. "How Prevalent Is Filovirus Exposure Worldwide?" <u>Outbreak:</u>

<u>Ebola Science and Medicine.</u> Ed. David Omstein. 1996. 30 Dec. 1998

<http://outbreak.org/cgi-unreg/dynaserve.exe/Ebola/ebola-

prevalence.html>.

Author's name (if known). Title of article (in quotation marks). Website (underlined). Editor of Website (if given). Web publication date. Date you accessed the file. Full Internet address (in angle brackets).

In-text Citation

"Filoviruses are present worldwide and vary in their ability to cause disease"

(Axton).

Online Magazine

Works Cited Entry

Kunen, James S. "The Test of Their Lives." <u>Time</u> 16 June 1997. 20 June 1997

<http://www.pathfinder.com/@@3iQRBQUAOc6Z09Xh/time/

magazine/1997/ >.

Author's name (if given). Title of article (in quotation marks). Name of the magazine (underlined). Date of magazine. Date you accessed the file. Full Internet address (in angle brackets).

In-text Citation

While high school exit exams have raised the standards of education in many

states, it has exacted a high price for some children who have difficulty with test

taking (Kunen).

Documentation
Internet

Online Newspaper or News Service

Works Cited Entry

"Gov.-elect Bush Makes Another Round of Appointments." <u>Miami Herald</u> 30 Dec.

1998. 30 Dec. 1998 <http://www.miamiherald.com/docs/089529.htm>.

Author (if given). Article (in quotation marks). Name of newspaper or News Service (underlined). Date of publication. Number of pages or paragraphs, if numbered. Date you accessed the article. Full Internet address (in angle brackets).

In-Text Citation

The <u>Miami Herald</u> reported that Governor Elect Jeb Bush has appointed Michael

Moore to run the Florida Prison System ("Gov.-elect Bush").

Electronic Text (e. g. Book, Poem, Short Story)

Works Cited Entry

Washington, Booker T. <u>Up From Slavery: An Autobiography.</u> Garden City, NY:

Doubleday, 1901. <u>Documenting the American South: Beginnings to</u>

<u>1920.</u> 19 Sept. 1998. U. of North Carolina-Chapel Hill. 15 Jan. 1999

<http://metalab.unc.edu/docsouth/washington/title.html>.

Author (if given). If the work is a poem or short story, place it in quotation marks; if it is a book, underline the title. Publication information for work (if given). Project name (underlined). Editor of the project (if given). Web publication date (if given). Physical location of project. Date you accessed the data. Full Internet address of the work (in angle brackets).

In-text Citation

Booker T. Washington felt that slavery "was so constructed as to cause labour, as

a rule, to be looked upon as a badge of degradation, of inferioritiy."

Specialized Online Database or Subscription Service (e.g. Electric Library)

Works Cited Entry

Newton, Jim and Eric Malvic. "Police Sources Link Evidence to Simpson." <u>Los</u>

<u>Angeles Times</u> 15 June 1994: A1. Dialog. Swain County High School

Lib., Bryson City, NC. 10 May 1995 <http://www.dialog.com/>.

Author's name. Title and publication data for print source. Database
Provider. Physical place where you accessed the file. Date you
accessed the file. Complete Internet address (in angle brackets).

In-text Citation

Physical evidence linking Simpson to the crime include bloodstains in one of

Simpson's cars, a bloodstained glove found at Simpson's mansion and rust-colored

spots believed to be blood on his driveway (Newton and Malvic).

E-Mail
With Subject Line

Works Cited Entry

Massengil, Laura. "Re: Embroidery." E-mail to Janice Marsh. 28 May 1998.

Without Subject Line

Smith, Carl. E-mail to the author. 16 Mar. 1998.

Name of person sending e-mail. Subject of e-mail (if given). Recipient of
the E-mail. Date of message.

In-text Citation

When working with silk thread, knotting on the underside of the fabric may be

tedious (Massengil).

Documentation
Internet

Online Television or Radio Program

Works Cited Entry

Flatow, Ira. "Hour One: Christmas Science: Astronomy and Reindeer." <u>Science</u>

<u>Friday</u>. National Public Radio. 25 Dec. 1998. 30 Dec. 1998 <http://

www.sciencefriday.com/pages/1998/Dec/hour 1_122598.html>.

*Host or editor. Title of segment (in quotation marks). Name of Program
(underlined). Network. Date of broadcast. Date you accessed
the site. Full Internet address (in angle brackets).*

In-Text Citation

Most experts agree that reindeer and caribou are of the same species even though

they do not look alike (Flatow).

Sound Clip

Works Cited Entry

Einstein, Albert. "Einstein Speaks on the Fate of the European Jews." Voice of

America, 10 Dec. 1945. <u>A. Einstein: Image and Impact.</u> 1 Jan. 1999

<http://www.aip.org/history/einstein/voice2.htm>.

*Composer, conductor or performer. Title of work (in quotation marks).
Original source of work (if given). Date of original work (if
given). Name of website (underlined). Date you accessed the
site. Full Internet address (in angle brackets).*

In-Text Citation

Note: You may be using the contents of this sound clip within a document or you

may be using the sound clip itself within a presentation. If you use this material

within a written document, credit should be given to the source by citing the

creator's last name or the sound clip title within the in-text citation. If you are

using the sound clip in an oral presentation, credit should be given to the sound

clip within the credits at the end of the presentation.

Film Clip

Works Cited Entry

Leaving Port. 1998. Titantic. 1 Jan. 1999 <http://www.titanicmovie.com/>.

Director. Title of film clip (underlined). Date of film clip (if given). Title of film (underlined). Date you accessed the site. Full Internet address (in angle brackets).

In-Text Citation

Note: You may be using the contents of this film clip within a document or you may be using the film clip itself within a presentation. If you use this material within a written document, credit should be given to the source by citing the director's last name where available or the film clip title within the in-text citation. If you are using the film clip in an oral presentation, credit should be given to the film clip within the credits at the end of the presentation.

Image

Works Cited Entry

Cunninghame, R. J. "The First Bull Elephant." photograph. 1909. Smithsonian

Institution Archives, Washington, D. C. 31 Jan. 1999 <http://

www.npg.si.edu:80/exh/roosevelt/elephant.htm>.

Creator of work (if given). Title of work or identifying criteria (in quotation marks). Media type. Year created. Name of website where image was found (underlined). Location of website. Date of access. Full Internet address (in angle brackets).

In-Text Citation

Note: The image should be linked within the document to the Creator of the image wherever possible or by name or by the identifying criteria.

A ROOKIE'S GUIDE TO RESEARCH

Basic Research Paper

This chapter will show samples of

Rocky Mountain Spotted Fever

by

Mary K. Lindsay

Biology

Mrs. Clapsaddle

1 May 1997

*The **title page** is optional since the necessary information is repeated on the first page of the research paper; however, if your instructor requires one, the format shown here is acceptable.*

Rocky Mountain Spotted Fever

Thesis: The purpose of this paper is to define and give statistics about Rocky Mountain

Spotted Fever; describe its symptoms, diagnosis and treatment; and relate

preventive measures and the future outlook of the disease.

I. Definition and statistics of Rocky Mountain Spotted Fever

A. Definition

B. Statistics

1. Where RMSF is found

2. Number of cases

3. Number of deaths

II. Symptoms

A. High fever

B. Rash

C. Other symptoms

1. Joint and muscle pain

2. Nausea

3. More serious problems

III. Diagnosis and treatment

A. Diagnosis

1. Suspected tick bite

2. Medical tests

B. Treatment

Basic Research Paper Outline

IV. Prevention and future outlook

    A. Prevention

        1. Protective clothing

        2. Self-examination

    B. Future outlook

Margins:
Top: 1/2 inch
Bottom: 1 inch
Left and Right:
1 inch

Title *is centered two lines below the date. It is not typed in all capitals; it is not placed in larger type; it is not surrounded by quotation marks.*

First Page information:
Name
Class
Teacher
Date
(Note that the day comes first)

Introductory Paragraph

Definition

Do not refer to an item by an abbreviation without first letting the reader know what the abbreviation represents. This should be done the first time the abbreviation is mentioned.

Page number *is placed 1/2 inch from the top margin and 1 inch from the right edge of the paper. Your last name precedes the page number.*

Thesis Statement

Teachers may allow beginning research writers to use this form for the thesis statement to help clarify the different points to be covered in the paper; however, as you gain experience in writing papers, you should refine your thesis sentence.

Lindsay 1

Mary K. Lindsay

Biology

Mrs. Clapsaddle

1 May 1997

Rocky Mountain Spotted Fever

When we consider all the things that can happen to us, we are indeed lucky if we never experience a serious accident, illness, or disease. One unexpected disease that people sometimes contract in the spring or early summer is Rocky Mountain Spotted Fever. The purpose of this paper is to define and give statistics about Rocky Mountain Spotted Fever; describe its symptoms, diagnosis and treatment; and relate preventive measures and the future outlook of the disease.

What is Rocky Mountain Spotted Fever? It is "an acute infectious disease that is sometimes fatal" (Mactire 80). People get it from tick bites; several species of ticks transmit the bacteria Rickettsia which causes the disease. Rocky Mountain Spotted Fever (RMSF) was first found in the Rocky Mountain states (hence its name) less than a hundred years ago. At that time mortality from the disease was high, and its cause was unknown (Wilson and Sinert). Now, it is found in many more places; in fact, forty-six different states have reported cases. The Southern Atlantic states report more cases than the Western Mountain states; more than "half the cases in the United States occur in Maryland, Virginia, North Carolina, and Georgia" (Mactire 80). Between 600 and 1,200 cases of RMSF are reported each year. People still die from the disease, but there are fewer fatalities because of modern treatment. "The average mortality has been reduced from 25% to 5%" (Moore and Quick).

Basic Research Paper
Page 2

*Use a **basic font** such as Times New Roman to type your report. Never use a script font. **12 point type** is standard.*

When two or more references in the list of works cited begin with the same word, additional word/words should be added to identify which entry the in-text documentation references.

Follow each step in your outline as you discuss each element of the paper.

Lindsay 2

Certain signs and symptoms indicate that one might have RMSF. First, a very rapid onset of fever occurs in almost all patients. Somewhere between one to fifteen days after the fever appears, 85% to 90% of the infected people develop a rash. This rash appears first on the wrists, ankles, palms, soles, and forearms. It then spreads rapidly over the rest of the body (Moore and Quick). Joint and muscle pain, nausea, and chills are other symptoms. The heart, liver, lungs, and kidneys begin to show damage if treatment is not started soon enough. "The blood may flow around the body so slowly that gangrene develops in the fingers and toes" ("Rocky," Marshall 640).

How is RMSF diagnosed? First, anyone who experiences any of the above-mentioned symptoms within two weeks after removing a tick should immediately go to a doctor ("Rocky," Healthbeat). In fact, because tick bites are painless, a victim may never discover the feasting insect; therefore, even though a person doesn't know he has been bitten by a tick but experiences symptoms such as those described above, he should quickly seek medical treatment (Moore and Quick).

Several different medical tests are available to diagnose RMSF and differentiate it from similar diseases. Because of its low cost, one test widely used for detection of RMSF is the Weil-Felix test; however, in their article Moore and Quick suggest that newer, more sensitive tests are more reliable (n. pag.). A doctor "may do a blood test to confirm the diagnosis or may stain a specimen of the rash to detect the presence of the causative organism" (Larson 855). Whether a specific test is used or if diagnosis is made based on clinical symptoms and knowledge of being tick-bitten, the important thing is to have the diagnosis confirmed as quickly as possible so that treatment can begin. Postponement of medical help greatly increases the possibility of

*Use **numerals** when indicating percents; spell out numbers that can be written in one or two words.*

*Your entire paper, including the list of Works Cited, should be **double-spaced.***

*When the authors are mentioned in the text (a **"signal phrase"**), the page number is all that is required for the in-text citation. Since this entry has no page numbers, including **n. pag.** (no pagination) prevents misinterpretation.*

*Internal citation for **work by two authors***

Lindsay 3

death (Moore and Quick).

Effective treatments for RMSF were first discovered in the early 1950s. Treatment with the antibiotics chloramphenicol and tetracycline have proven highly effective. Usually, after treatment with tetracycline antibiotics, a person begins to improve dramatically with death occurring in 5 - 7% of cases; these deaths usually result from people delaying treatment ("Rocky," Health Answers). For those who cannot tolerate oral medication, chloramphenicol IV is effective. Both of these medications can also be used with younger children, but a woman who is pregnant should not be given these antibiotics. Again, the main thing to remember concerning treatment is to get it as soon as possible; even a short delay can mean the difference between life and death (Mactire 81).

Prevention of RMSF consists of one thing: a person must not receive a tick bite; however, this is sometimes more difficult than it sounds unless one is willing to lock himself inside from spring through early summer—and even this is not a guarantee against infection. Proper clothing, therefore, becomes the first line of prevention when one is in tick-infested areas. One should wear clothing that completely covers the body and fits snugly at the wrists, ankles, and waist. Also, "each outer garment should overlap the one above . . ." ("Rocky," medaccess). Secondly, self-examination allows a person to spot a tick so that it can be promptly removed. Most ticks do not attach quickly and seldom transmit disease unless attached for four or more hours ("Rocky," Healthbeat)

One must be very careful in detaching a tick that is visible under the skin so that the complete pest is removed. Placing a drop of alcohol or the head of a just-

No page number is required for Internet source.

Period follows the parenthesis *in the internal citation. If the cited material ends in a question mark or an explanation point, place them before the beginning parenthesis. Place a period at the end of the parenthesis, however. Example: . . . answer? (Johns 83).*

*An **ellipse** is used to indicate that words have been omitted within a quotation.*

Basic Research Paper
Page 4

Lindsay 4

extinguished match on the area will loosen the tick's hold. Then, one can use a pair of tweezers to remove it, being very careful not to crush it. Another method used to extract the tick is to cover it with petroleum jelly for at least twenty minutes. This procedure suffocates the tick which can then be removed with tweezers ("Rocky," Marshall 640).

Questions can be an effective means of providing transitions between parts of your paper.

What is the future outlook for RMSF? Chemical pesticides are available for reducing the tick population in areas of great infestation, but there are serious drawbacks to using them. For one thing, their high cost prevents most individuals or agencies from considering them. Too, many of these pesticides cause potential harm to the environment, and this possible damage outweighs the good of eradicating the ticks. It is also interesting to note that until about eight years ago there was a vaccine available; however, because it gave very limited protection, it was taken off the market and additional vaccines have not been developed ("Rocky," medaccess).

An appropriate conclusion is necessary. It should summarize the information you presented and/or restate the thesis sentence.

In conclusion, RMSF is a very serious disease that can cause death. Fortunately, its symptoms are usually easy to identify and, with quick diagnosis, effective treatment is possible. Diligent attention to the possibility of tick bites is the best prevention to assure that a person does not have to contend with this possibly fatal disease.

*When citing a work with an **anonymous author**, use only enough words of the title to identify the source. When more than one source begins with the same word/s, additional words should be added to distinguish which source was used.*

The words "Works Cited" should appear at the top of the page. They should not be typed in all capital letters and should not be printed in bold face type.

The page containing the list of works cited is also numbered.

Lindsay 5

Works Cited

The first line of each citation begins at the left margin. Additional lines should be indented five spaces from the left margin.

Larson, David E., ed. The Mayo Clinic Family Health Book. New York: Morrow, 1990.

Mactire, Sean P. Lyme Disease and Other Pest-Borne Illnesses. New York: Franklin

Watts, 1992.

Generally page numbers are not required for books in the list of works cited.

Moore, Lloyd, and Gary Quick. "Tick-borne Diseases: Rocky Mountain Spotted Fever

and Lyme Disease are Still in Season." Consultant Aug. 1994: 1203-10. InfoTrac:

Health Reference Center. CD-ROM. Information Access. Feb. 1997.

Alphabetize each entry in the list of works cited. If no author is given, alphabetize by the first word of the article or book unless the first word is A, An or The. In these instances, alphabetize by the first main word of the work.

"Rocky Mountain Spotted Fever." 8 Apr. 1997 <http://www.medaccess.com/physical/

inf-dis/rmsf.htm>.

When internet sources have incomplete data, use only what is available.

"Rocky Mountain Spotted Fever." Health Answers. 1998. 8 Jan. 1999 <http://

www.healthanswers.com/database/ami/converted/000654.html>.

"Rocky Mountain Spotted Fever." Healthbeat: Illinois Department of Public Health.

1998. 12 Jan. 1999 <http://www.idph.state.il.us/public/hb/hbrmsf.htm>.

"Rocky Mountain Spotted Fever." The Marshall Cavendish Encyclopedia of Health.

Vol. 11. North Biltmore, New York: Cavendish, 1991, 14 vols.

Citations should match standard formats in capitalization, punctuation and spacing. Do not deviate from the standards.

Wilson, Michael, and Richard Sinert. "Tick Diseases, Rocky Mountain Spotted Fever."

emedicine. Ed. Gary Setnik. 23 Sept. 1998. 12 Jan. 1999 <www.emedicine.com/

emerg/topic510.htm>.

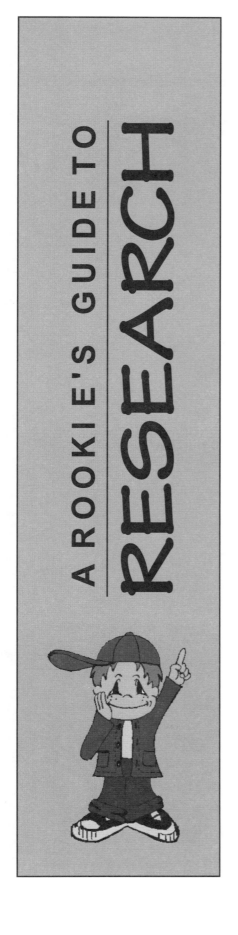

A ROOKIE'S GUIDE TO **RESEARCH**

Advanced Research Paper

This chapter will show samples of

Bruno Richard Hauptmann—Guilty or Innocent?

By

Mary K. Lindsay

U. S. Studies

Mrs. Clemens

1 April 1997

*The **title page** is optional since the necessary information is repeated on the first page of the research paper; however, if your instructor requires one, the format shown here is acceptable.*

Although a thesis sentence is not required on the outline page, students may organize their notes more effectively if it is included here.

Bruno Richard Hauptmann—Guilty or Innocent?

Thesis: Circumstantial evidence presented at the trial provides grounds for doubting the validity of Hauptmann's verdict.

Note order and format of outline.

I. Background

   A. The Lindberghs

   B. Kidnapping and investigation

      1. Events on night of 1 March 1932

      2. Ransom payment

      3. Arrest of Bruno Richard Hauptmann

II. Major evidence presented against Hauptmann

   A. Hidden ransom money

   B. Ladder used in kidnapping

   C. Witnesses

      1. John Condon

      2. Taxi driver Perrone

      3. Amandus Hochmath

      4. Charles Lindbergh

   D. Ransom notes

   E. Two other pieces of evidence

      1. Phone number in closet

      2. Work sheets

III. Examination of evidence

   A. Ransom money

   B. Ladder

Advanced Research Paper Outline

      C. Witnesses

      D. Ransom notes

      E. Phone number and work sheets

      F. Other facts to consider

          1. Lack of fingerprints

          2. Lack of knowledge of Lindbergh living arrangements

          3. Hauptmann's refusal to confess

IV. Questioning validity of the case

      A. Kennedy's <u>The Airman and the Carpenter</u>

      B. Anna Hauptmann's life-long defense of husband

      C. Scaduto's <u>Scapegoat</u>

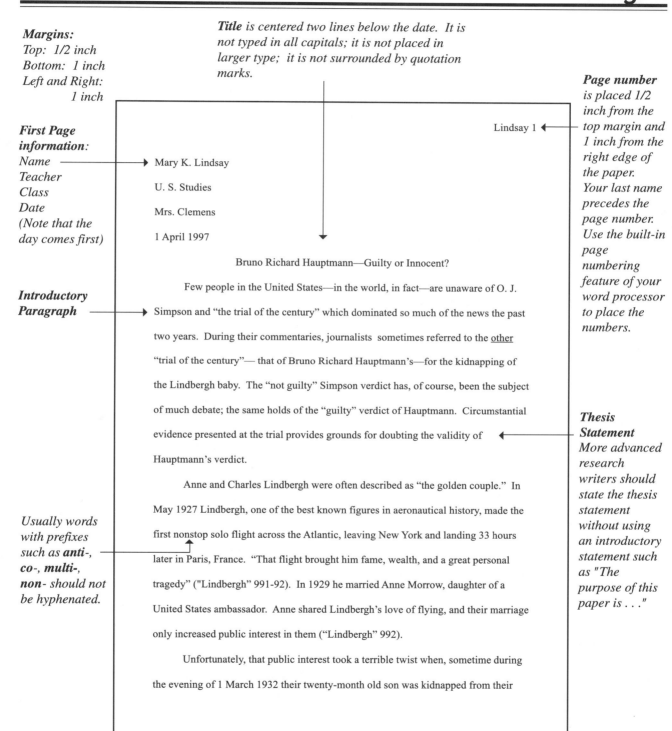

Margins:
Top: 1/2 inch
Bottom: 1 inch
Left and Right:
*   1 inch*

Title is centered two lines below the date. It is not typed in all capitals; it is not placed in larger type; it is not surrounded by quotation marks.

Page number *is placed 1/2 inch from the top margin and 1 inch from the right edge of the paper. Your last name precedes the page number. Use the built-in page numbering feature of your word processor to place the numbers.*

First Page information:
Name
Teacher
Class
Date
(Note that the day comes first)

Introductory Paragraph

Usually words with prefixes such as anti-, co-, multi-, non- should not be hyphenated.

Thesis Statement *More advanced research writers should state the thesis statement without using an introductory statement such as "The purpose of this paper is . . ."*

Lindsay 1

Mary K. Lindsay

U. S. Studies

Mrs. Clemens

1 April 1997

Bruno Richard Hauptmann—Guilty or Innocent?

Few people in the United States—in the world, in fact—are unaware of O. J. Simpson and "the trial of the century" which dominated so much of the news the past two years. During their commentaries, journalists sometimes referred to the other "trial of the century"— that of Bruno Richard Hauptmann's—for the kidnapping of the Lindbergh baby. The "not guilty" Simpson verdict has, of course, been the subject of much debate; the same holds of the "guilty" verdict of Hauptmann. Circumstantial evidence presented at the trial provides grounds for doubting the validity of Hauptmann's verdict.

Anne and Charles Lindbergh were often described as "the golden couple." In May 1927 Lindbergh, one of the best known figures in aeronautical history, made the first nonstop solo flight across the Atlantic, leaving New York and landing 33 hours later in Paris, France. "That flight brought him fame, wealth, and a great personal tragedy" ("Lindbergh" 991-92). In 1929 he married Anne Morrow, daughter of a United States ambassador. Anne shared Lindbergh's love of flying, and their marriage only increased public interest in them ("Lindbergh" 992).

Unfortunately, that public interest took a terrible twist when, sometime during the evening of 1 March 1932 their twenty-month old son was kidnapped from their

Advanced Research Paper
Page 2

*Use a **basic font** such as Times New Roman to type your report. Never use a script font or one that is difficult to read. 12 point type is standard.*

home near Hopewell, New Jersey. A quick search revealed mud on the nursery floor, a broken ladder underneath the window as well as some footprints, and a ransom note demanding $50,000. During the ensuing weeks other ransom notes were received, most of them through John Condon, an intermediary chosen by the kidnapper. The ransom demands were delivered to Condon by a man who identified himself as "John." More than 70 days after the kidnapping, the child's body was accidentally discovered near a roadway some four miles from the Lindbergh home. A blow to the head, probably occurring the night he was taken, had killed the baby ("Bruno").

Internet sources do not require page numbers in the internal documentation.

Follow your outline step-by-step as you develop your paper.

The intensity of the investigation then turned toward discovering the killer(s) of the child. Months elapsed without substantial evidence, and it wasn't until September 1934 that thirty-two year old Bruno Richard Hauptmann was arrested. Twelve years earlier Hauptmann, leaving his native Germany, stole on board a ship for America and jumped over the side to reach land, hoping for a better life in the United States (Kennedy 66-68). On 2 January 1935 his trial, termed even then "the trial of the century," began (Oxford 66). Anyone familiar with the history of the case knows that Hauptmann was found guilty and executed for the crime. Over the decades, however, "post-trail investigations indicated grave flaws in the prosecution's case" (Cray, Kolter, and Better 227).

When the date is presented in this manner, no commas are required.

Example of internal documentation for a work by three authors.

The first major evidence against Hauptmann was the almost $12,000 found hidden in his garage. The police were certain that the money was indeed the ransom payment because the numbers of all the bills had been copied and distributed to the banks throughout the country before being given to the kidnapper ("Abduction"15). Hauptmann's explanation for his having the money was rather incredulous.

*Your entire paper, including the list of works cited, should be **double spaced**.*

*Figures which
are used
internally should
be labeled
consecutively
and identified.*

Lindsay 3

According to him, a business associate named Fisch, who he later learned was a con artist, gave him a shoe box, asking him to keep it for him until he returned from a visit to Germany. Fisch died there, and it was only when Hauptmann learned of his death that he remembered the box which he had placed in a kitchen closet. The box and its contents had gotten wet. Hauptmann dried out the money he discovered in the box, hid it in various places in the garage, and decided to keep it since Fisch owed him money (Ryan 389).

The second major piece of evidence was the ladder used to get into the nursery, a crudely built one made of eleven rungs and six side pieces. Arthur Koehler, head of the Forest Service Laboratory of the U.S. Department of Agriculture in Wisconsin, diligently studied the broken ladder piece by piece, numbering each part according to the figure below:

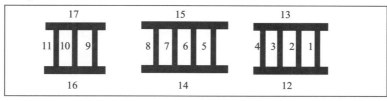

Figure 1 Ladder parts

He found section sixteen to be significantly different from the others; for instance, it was differently planed, was a poorer grade, was narrower, and had been stored indoors. Koehler actually traced that type of lumber to a South Carolina business, discovering that shipments had been sent to a lumberyard in the Bronx near where Hauptmann lived (Kennedy 144). Then, during the investigation, a Detective Bormann searched the attic of Hauptmann's house and discovered that a piece of flooring had been removed.

Lindsay 4

When information comes from different sources in one sentence, each source must be cited.

Koehler and he determined that section sixteen came from this missing area (Kennedy 211-13) and, during the trial, Koehler used blowups to show the similarities between section sixteen of the ladder and the remaining ends of the board in the attic, testifying that section sixteen was the missing link (Keller 18).

Documentation showing information from multiple pages.

Then, a parade of witnesses helped in the conviction. Dr. John Condon, the man used as a go-between, identified Hauptmann as the "John" to whom he gave the ransom. Perrone, a taxi driver to whom "John" gave a note to deliver to Condon, also pointed to Hauptmann (Kennedy 176-77). Next, eighty-seven year old Amandus Hochmath stated he saw Hauptmann driving his car with a ladder on top of it near the Lindbergh home the day before the kidnapping (Kennedy 215-16). Other witnesses were also called, but the most damaging testimony, because of the emotional impact, was Lindbergh's. On the night the money was passed from Condon to the kidnapper, Lindbergh was hidden in the background. He heard the kidnapper yell, "Hey, Doc." After his arrest, Hauptmann had been required to yell the same words in Lindbergh's presence; Lindbergh identified Hauptmann as "John" (Kennedy 218-19).

Adding to the growing body of evidence, the prosecutors used the ransom notes themselves to further their case. During the first days of his arrest Hauptmann had letters dictated to him to write; then he had actually been given copies of the ransom notes and told to copy them as exactly as he could. He stated, "I'll be glad to because it'll help get me out of this thing" (Kennedy 154). This, however, was not the case. The state called various handwriting experts to the stand where they used blowups of the notes and samples to show the similarities (Ryan 389).

Two other chief pieces of prosecution evidence also involved writing. On the

Note that the period follows the internal documentation. Quotation marks stay with the sentence, but a period still follows the parenthesis.

Lindsay 5

inside of a closet in the Hauptmann home, detectives found a phone number that seemed to have been there for some time. When asked if he had written the number there, Hauptmann said that, although he didn't recall doing so, he must have if the number existed. The number was that of Dr. John Condon (Kennedy 204). Too, on March 1, the Tuesday of the kidnapping, Hauptmann said he began a new job at the Majestic Apartments. The supervisor was uncertain of the exact date, and the work records, at least those which were not missing, indicated he started work at a later time (Davidson 28).

*Note the use of transitional phrases and words such as **then, other, adding** and **next** to link paragraphs together.*

Other evidence just as incriminating was presented during the trial and, on the surface, would make almost anyone consider Hauptmann guilty. At the time of the trial and in the ensuing years, however, several people questioned the validity of the evidence and either stated it to be false or at least misleading. For instance, as improbable as the shoe box story sounded, Hauptmann's best friend saw Fisch arrive at Hauptmann's house with a shoe box (Kennedy 243). A plumber named Miller testified that Hauptmann hired him to fix a leak in the closet, and a chemical analysis of the ransom money gave further proof that the money had at one time been wet (Kennedy 214). Even later, a United Press reporter named Sidney Whipple found a steamboat agent who remembered that Fisch paid for his travel ticket in $10 and $20 gold certificates, the type of money used to pay the ransom (Kennedy 154).

Notice that the author presents both sides of the evidence.

Another piece of vital evidence to be reexamined was the ladder. Although Detective Bornmann said he found a board missing from the attic floor of Hauptmann's house on his <u>second</u> visit, the prosecution did not put into the record the previous

Advanced Research Paper
Page 6

Lindsay 6

unsuccessful searches by others. Records show that during the five days before

Bornmann's discovery, thirty-seven policemen had made <u>nine</u> visits to the same attic

and found nothing. One investigator vows that "Section 16" fits only if one can

accept that several major gaps make no difference (Kennedy 213).

  Next, one by one, the reliability of the witnesses can be challenged. Although

Dr. Condon had seen the kidnapper several times, it was always at night with poor

lighting, and when he was asked to identify Hauptmann from a lineup, he did not do

so at the time. It was only later after the police had encouraged him that he did so on

the witness stand (Kennedy 192). Perrone, the taxi driver, had said on the night he

was handed the ransom note to deliver that he wouldn't be able to recognize the man

again yet, over two years later, he did identify Hauptmann (Kennedy 176-77).

Lindbergh, too, based his identification on two words heard more than two years

earlier. The old man who testified to seeing Hauptmann the day before the

kidnapping never once mentioned it to his daughter and son-in-law with whom he

was staying; in fact, he told no one until after a substantial reward was offered

(Kennedy 244).

  The writing matches also need to be examined carefully. The police had

Hauptmann write seven different versions of the ransom note using different pens; he

was to recreate as exactly as possible the style of writing and the spelling. Osborn, a

well known expert of that time, was called in to examine the writing. Sisk, a special

police agent, stated that Osborn went home and spent hours on his analysis and that

"after examining them for a while he found a lot of dissimilarities" and became

convinced he [Hauptmann] did not write the ransom notes (Kennedy 178). In 1982 a

Square brackets indicate wording that is not part of the original quotation.

66

*Use strong
verbs with
signal phrases
to project the
intended
meaning. See
list on page 80.*

*If a quotation is
more than four
lines in length,
double space
and indent the
entire citation
10 spaces from
the left margin.
Notice that the
period comes
before the in-
text citation
when the
quotation is
indented.*

Lindsay 7

British handwriting expert examined the handwriting evidence "in great detail"
(Kennedy 418).   He asserted:

> The differences between the ransom writing and Hauptmann's writing
>
> which have been pointed out in this report are very prominent and, I submit,
>
> far outweigh occasional similarities to which the reader's attention has been
>
> drawn . . . I conclude this summary by reaffirming my opinion that the
>
> ransom letters were not written by Hauptmann. (Kennedy 418)

Even more recently, during a television interview a forensic handwriting expert,

discussing a case in the news today in which a ransom note is involved, stated that,

though many similarities can exist, handwriting evidence is very often being

considered "inconclusive" (Good Morning).

Finally, problems arise with the phone number in the closet and the time sheets

for work. Although Hauptmann stated that he must have written Condon's number,

when he realized where it was actually located, he said he would never have put

something in writing there. Sometime after the execution it was learned that a

journalist named Tom Cassidy wrote the number in the closet—as a joke; but, since he

felt Hauptmann was guilty, he did not feel it necessary to let anyone know during the

trial. Three people who knew Cassidy confirmed that he told them of his involvement

(Kennedy 204). Supposedly nonexistent work sheets did exist for March 1-15, March

1 being the date of the kidnapping when Hauptmann said he was at work. The sheets

look altered; there are dots marking out checks showing Hauptmann worked those first

days of March (Kennedy 185). When first questioned, the construction supervisor, a

Mr. Furcht, stated that "on 1 March, 1932, at 8 a.m. Bruno Richard Hauptmann and

*Documentation
should follow
immediately
after a direct
quotation even
if the material
following it
comes from the
same source.*

*Example of
in-text
documentation
for a television
show.*

*Retain
punctuation in
the original
quotation even
if it is
incorrect.*

Lindsay 8

Gus Kassens reported to work at the Majestic Apartments and worked throughout the

entire day until five o'clock" (Kennedy 79). Inexplicably, it was only later that

Furcht said he couldn't remember the exact date that Hauptmann first came to work

(Kennedy 227).

Some other important facts also need to be addressed. Although hundreds of

fingerprints were found on the ladder, some of which were never identified, not one

match was ever made with Hauptmann's prints (Kennedy 87). Furthermore, how

could Hauptmann have known that the Lindberghs would be at their new home on

this particular night? The decision to stay had been made at the very last minute,

making this the <u>first</u> week night the Lindberghs spent in their new home. Only the

immediate family and a few servants knew of the changed plans (Mosley 186). Add

to this the fact that of the 50 windows in the new home, the only shutters that were

warped and would not lock were in the nursery (Groves). Finally, after the arrest the

police beat Hauptmann severely, yet he refused to confess (Kennedy 5). And, when it

was certain he would die for the crime, the <u>New York Evening Journal</u> offered to

write a $75,000 check to his wife Anna if he would tell his story to them. Again, he

refused, although his great love for his wife and young son was evident and he knew

that he would be leaving them destitute (Oxford 69).

Since Hauptmann's death in 1936, a mass of writing on the kidnapping and

trial has been published. One detailed book that examines the court evidence is

Ludovic Kennedy's <u>The Airman and the Carpenter.</u> Reviewing Kennedy's 1985 book,

Prescott notes that "in recent decades . . . many have doubted that justice was served

by Hauptmann's execution in 1936" (73). Furthermore, he points out that in writing

When the author's name is used in a "signal phrase", only the page number should be cited.

Advanced research papers require hard proof to back up a thesis. Citing additional sources which support your stand can help make your thesis more believable.

Lindsay 9

An ellipse (. . .) shows that some of the quoted data has been omitted.

his book Kennedy wasn't impartial, often using an offensive tone, but, "in the end he

makes his case . . . the accumulated weight of these facts argues persuasively for

Hauptmann's innocence" (73).

No one believed more firmly in the innocence of Bruno Richard Hauptmann than

his wife Anna Hauptmann. Until her death at the age of 96 in October 1994, she

declared that justice had not been served. She spent much of her life in "a vain quest to

exonerate her husband ("Anna Hauptmann").

A CD-ROM source does not require a page number in the documentation.

Conclusion restates the thesis sentence and summarizes the arguments that have been made by the researcher.

In writing of a 1976 book entitled Scapegoat, the reviewer stated that "despite the

unearthing of considerable discrepancies . . . Scaduto [the author] failed to present solid

proof that Hauptmann was the victim of a miscarriage of justice" (Sifakis 431). If

"solid proof" means the specific identification of the real kidnapper, the reviewer is

correct; however, numerous articles have been written about the case using the term

"circumstantial evidence" to explain Hauptmann's conviction. Could not the

"circumstantial evidence" written about in this paper also be used to prove the man's

innocence? Shortly before his death, Hauptmann wrote to the state's prosecutor:

Note that this conclusion repeats the basic thesis without restating it word for word.

> Mr. Wilentz, with my dying breath, I swear by God that you convicted an
>
> innocent man. Once you will stand before the same judge to whom I go in a
>
> few hours. You know you have done wrong on me,[sic] you will not only
>
> take my life but also all the happiness of my family. God will be judge
>
> between me [sic] and you. I beg you, Attorney General, believe at least a
>
> dying man. Please investigate, because this case is not solved, it only adds
>
> another dead [sic] to the Lindbergh case. (Kennedy 394)

The bracketed word [sic] is used to indicate an error such as grammar or spelling in the original source.

In a long quotation, the punctuation follows the quotation rather than the citation.

Perhaps it is the plea of this dying man to "please investigate" that causes people even

today to search for the whole truth.

Advanced Research Paper
Works Cited

The words "Works Cited" should be centered one inch from the top of page.

All entries in the list of works cited are placed in alphabetical order by author or by the first main word of the entry.

The list of works cited should always begin on a separate page.

Note that the works cited entries are double spaced and that the page is numbered consecutively.

Identify the town in which the newspaper is published when its name is not given within the newspaper's name.

The first line of each entry begins at the left margin with each additional line indented five spaces.

Lindsay 10

Works Cited

"Abduction: The Lindbergh Baby." Crimes and Punishment: The Illustrated Crimes Encyclopedia. Vol. 1. Westport, Ct.: Stuttman, 1994. 28 vols.

"Anna Hauptmann." Time 31 Oct. 1994: 24. InfoTrac: SuperTOM+. CD-ROM, Information Access. Jan. 1997.

"Bruno Richard Hauptmann, Kidnaping [sic] and Murder of Charles A. Lindbergh, Jr." Federal Bureau of Investigation Homepage. 25 Jan. 1999 <http://www.fbi.gov/ famcases/hauptman.htm>.

Cray, Ed, Jonathan Kotler, and Miles Better. American Datelines. New York: Facts on File, 1990.

Davidson, David. "The Story of the Century." American Heritage 27: 2 (1976): 22-29.

Good Morning America. American Broadcasting Company. WJLA, Washington, D.C. 20 Mar. 1997.

Groves, Bob. "The Case Against Lindbergh." The Record (Hackensack, N.J.) 18 Apr. 1993: L1+. History. Ed. Eleanor Goldstein. Boca Raton, Fl: SIRS, 1993. Art. 64.

Keller, Allan. "The Baby is Found. . .Dead." American History Illustrated 10:2 (1975): 10-21.

Kennedy, Ludovic. The Airman and the Carpenter. New York: Viking, 1985.

"Lindbergh, Charles." Encyclopaedia Britannica. 1975 ed.

Mosley, Leonard. Lindbergh: A Biography. New York: Doubleday, 1966.

Oxford, Edward. "The Other Trial of the Century." American History July 1995: 18+. InfoTrac: SuperTOM+. CD-ROM, Information Access. Jan. 1997.

Lindsay 11

Prescott, Peters. "Cobbling Up a Conviction." <u>Newsweek</u> 24 June 1985: 73.

Ryan, Bernard, Jr. "Bruno Richard Hauptmann Trial: 1935." <u>Great American Trials</u>.

      Ed. Edward W. Knappman. Detroit: Visible Ink, 1994.

Sifakis, Carl. "Lindbergh Kidnaping." <u>The Encyclopedia of American Crime</u>. New

      York: Smithmark, 1992.

A ROOKIE'S GUIDE TO RESEARCH

Appendix

In this section you will find

Directions

Begin by reading through the entire checklist. Although as a "rookie researcher", you may not understand the list, it will give you a "feel" for what is expected. After reading it through once, concentrate on the first section only. Check off each item as you complete it. Do not move on to the next section until you completely finish the current one. Permission is granted to reproduce pages 75-78 for classroom use.

Step One: Getting started

_____ 1. I have a supply of note cards and a folder in which to keep my materials.

_____ 2. I understand exactly what the assignment requires.

_____ 3. The topic I have chosen is appropriate (not too broad, too limited, too ordinary) for this particular assignment.

_____ 4. I have a list of questions that I can research on the topic which may possibly become the subtopics of my outline.

_____ 5. I have a working/preliminary thesis sentence which gives me direction for my research.

Step Two: Researching the topic

_____ 6. I have checked the library for all possible sources of information.

_____ 7. I have written down **all** the necessary information for the list of Works Cited page for each source I have consulted.

_____ 8. I have completed extensive reading/research on my topic.

_____ 9. I have taken many notes, writing only one idea on each note card.

_____ 10. I have identified the source (and page number if there is one) for each note card I have written.

_____ 11. I have identified a category (a slug) for each of my note cards.

_____ 12. I have put most of the information into my own words.

Appendix
Writer's Checklist

_____ 13. I have indicated direct quotations from sources by using quotation marks.

_____ 14. As I have read and taken notes, I have added to my list of questions (my preliminary outline) any new information that I have gathered.

_____ 15. I have sorted my note cards into groups according to categories (slugs).

Step Three: Composing the paper

_____ 16. I have a finished outline based on the information on my note cards.

_____ 17. I have completed a correct *Works Cited* page.

_____ 18. I have completed a "rough draft".

Step Four: Evaluating the rough draft

_____ 19. My paper begins with an introductory paragraph that creates interest in my topic.

_____ 20. My thesis is clearly stated in the introductory paragraph.

_____ 21. Each paragraph begins with a topic sentence.

_____ 22. I have used transitional words and phrases throughout the paper to add smoothness and to link information.

_____ 23. I have used strong action verbs. See listing on page 76.

_____ 24. I have placed quotation marks around data that was quoted directly as it was in the source.

_____ 25. I have documented (cited) the sources where my information was found originally.

_____ 26. I have sufficient details to support my points.

_____ 27. I have a conclusion that reinterates the thesis sentence.

Step Five:
Completing the
final draft

_____ 27. I have read the paper aloud to myself to check for errors

_____ 28. I have double-checked my paper for the following grammatical
errors:

   _____ Sentence fragments or run-ons

   _____ Proper capitalization

   _____ Correct subject-verb agreement

   _____ Consistent verb tense

   _____ Use of active voice verbs

   _____ Agreement of pronoun antecedents

   _____ Correct case of pronouns

   _____ Proper placement of punctuation marks

   _____ Apostrophe use

   _____ Commonly misspelled words: there, their, etc.

   _____ Spelling out numbers where indicated

   _____ Use of underlining and quotation marks

   _____ Misplaced modifiers

   _____ Redundancy

   _____ Deadwood or flowery language

   _____ Slang

_____ 29. I have run a spell check on the computer.

_____ 30. I have had someone else read my paper for errors.

_____ 31. I have used the correct formatting on every page.

_____ 32. I have arranged all of the material required by my instructor in a
neat and logical order.

Appendix
Research Paper Evaluation

This page may be used as an indicator as to how your instructor might evaluate your paper. Obviously, each instructor has his/her own grading criteria and he/she may place more emphasis on one area than we suggest.

Content: 30 points
_____ Points

- paper develops a thesis statement
- notecards or other forms of notetaking form basis for information
- writer used details, examples, etc. to support his viewpoints
- paper meets minimum requirements for length

COMMENT:_____

_____

Organization: 30 points
_____ Points

- paper contains an acceptable outline
- paper content follows outline
- writing sequences are clear and unified
- introductory paragraph is appealing and contains thesis sentence
- transitional words are used to produce smoothness

COMMENT:_____

_____

Formatting and grammar: 40 points
_____ Points

- in-text citations are done properly throughout the paper
- the list of works cited is typed and formatted correctly
- margins, page number placement, first page information, etc. are correct
- paper meets minimum requirement for number of references
- paper shows overall neatness
- correct punctuation and capitalization are used
- correct spelling and grammar are used
- sentence structure is varied

COMMENT:_____

_____

| Transitions | To move from one part of writing -- from one sentence to another, one paragraph to another, or even one chapter to another -- a good writer uses transitional words, phrases, and even sentences and paragraphs to assure smoothness and continuity. Below, you will find a list of transitional words. You will notice that they have been divided into groups based on usage. |

Time

before	meanwhile	as soon as	then
finally	immediately	during	later
as yet	until	tomorrow	after
next	yesterday	still	first
second			

Place

above	to the right/left	between	near
around	beyond	at the bottom	beside
next	throughout	in the center of	

Comparison/contrast

similarly	in the same way	although	also
however	but	by contrast	too
on the other hand			

Supporting and adding to

for example	in addition	for instance	such as
furthermore	together with	according to	likewise
what's more			

Emphasis

for this reason	in fact	likewise	thus
equally important			

Summarizing

finally	in conclusion	thus	therefore
consequently	in summary	as a result	

Appendix
Strong Verbs

Using strong verbs within your paper will make your viewpoint much more convincing and interesting. This is especially true as you use verbs with signal phrases to introduce a quotation. The list of verbs which follows is useful in making your paper say exactly what you wamt it to. They will enhance your writing and make the meaning of your sentences clearer. Be sure you know what the verb means before you use it, because some of the verbs promote either a negative or a positive image.

Strong Verbs

accentuates
acknowledges
admits
alleges
alludes to
argues
attests
authenticates
concedes
contrasts
contradicts
contends
corroborates
concedes
declares
determines
differs
disproves
disputes
emphasizes
endorses
equates
examines
expresses

gives credence
holds
indicates
infers
makes clear
maintains
marks
mentions
perceives
proves
quotes
relates
reviews
speculates
states
stresses
suggests
supports
underscores
validates
verifies
voices

Abbreviations often used in documentations

Common Abbreviations

anon.	anonymous
ch., chs.	chapter(s)
col., cols.	column(s)
ed., eds.	edition(s), editor(s), edited by
e. g.	for example
et al.	*et alii* ("and others")
illus.	illustrated by, illustrator, illustration(s)
l., ll.	line(s)
n. d.	no date (of publication)
no., nos.	number(s)
n.p.	no place (of publication), no publisher
n. pag.	no pagination
par.	paragraph
rev.	revision, revised by
rpt.	reprint, reprinted
sec.	section
trans.	translator, translated by
univ.	university
vol. vols.	volume(s)